T0060407

colorful creatures

stickers and activities

colorful creatures

stickers and activities

Anita Ganeri and Penny Arlon

weldonowen

weldon**owen**

Authors: Anita Ganeri and Penny Arlon

Design: Tory Gordon-Harris, Natalie Schmidt, Anna Pond

Editorial: Lydia Halliday, Susie Rae

Fact checker: Tom Jackson

Art Director: Stuart Smith

Publisher: Sue Grabham

Insight Editions Publisher: Raoul Goff

All photographs in this book including those used on the cover are used under license from Shutterstock.com with the following exceptions:
Page 10, "Crab" © chiravan39/iStock
Page 36, "Pygmy Blue Whale" © Franco Banfi/naturepl.com

Copyright © Weldon Owen International, L.P. 2021

All rights reserved. No part of this publication may be reproduced, distributed, or transmitted in any form or by any means, including photocopying, recording, or other electronic or mechanical methods, without the prior written permission of the publisher, except in the case of brief quotations embodied in critical reviews and certain other noncommercial uses permitted by copyright law.

Published by Weldon Owen Children's Books

An imprint of Weldon Owen International, L.P.

A subsidiary of Insight International, L.P.

PO Box 3088
San Rafael, CA 94912

www.insighteditions.com

ISBN: 978-1-68188-740-1

Printed in China

First printed in 2020

24 23 22 21 20 1 2 3 4 5

Contents

	Hello Color	6
	Red	8
	Orange	18
	Yellow	28
	Green	38
	Blue	48
	Pink and Purple	58
	Brown	68
	Black, White, and Grey	76
	Multi-colored	94
	Color Works	104

Look for the fun activities in each chapter. There are mazes, dot to dots, word searches, sticker scenes, and more!

Find the giant poster and sticker sheets at the end of the book!

Hello Color

Red, yellow, brown, pink, purple, blue, and orange—animals come in all sorts of colors. Some animals are brightly colored while other animals are harder to spot. Their colors are not simply for showing off. In nature, colors and patterns help animals to stay alive.

Some colors help animals to blend into the background for protection. While certain colors help animals to send signals to each other. This allows the animals to keep in touch and even find a mate. Bright colors are often warning signs that an animal tastes horrible or is poisonous.

Many animals have more than one color or pattern. They may be multicolored or have mixtures of stripes, splotches, and spots. These markings look strong and striking, but they also confuse attackers who find the animals difficult to see and catch. A few animals can even change color so that they can hide in different places, and also show their feelings.

In this book, you will meet animals of many colors, from striking black-and-white zebras to stunning emerald-green lizards. See if you can guess what they use their colors for.

Red

Many insects use mimicry to hide from predators or attract prey. This means they pretend to be something that they are not—like a disguise! The red leaf beetle, for example, is not poisonous, but a bird might avoid eating it because it looks similar to the poisonous ladybug.

Ladybugs
Grouper fish
Butterfly
Dart frog
Butterfly
Golden net-wing beetles
Scarlet lily beetle
Butterfly
Indonesian beetles
Butterfly
Milk snake
Butterfly
Red velvet mites
Bamboo snake
Firebug
Calico snake
Cardinal
Crab
Moontail bullseye fish
Seed tick
Bigeye fish
Red palm weevils

Betta fish
Bigeye fish
Australian king parrot
Indonesian beetle
Scarlet ibis
Potato beetle
Sea star
Scarlet lily beetle
Parrotfish
Ladybug
Stonefish
Betta fish
Cardinal lory
Sea star
Cichlid fish
Scarlet ibis
Butterfly
Red velvet mites
Seed ticks
Ladybird spider
Sea star
Bullfinch

Rooster
Red squirrel
Velvet ant
Betta fish
Strawberry finch
Bearded dragons
Ark clams
Bullfinch
Scallops
Monkfish
Great frigatebird
Velvet ants
Betta fish
Colorado beetles
Turkey
Milk snake
Sharp-nosed crab
Stag beetle
Hermit crab

Cardinal
Tomato frog
Lady beetles
Yellow-bibbed lory
Macaw
Panther chameleon
Firebugs
Butterfly
Mandrill
Coral snake
Sockeye salmon
Poplar leaf beetle
Red snappers

Get ready for these bright red puzzles. But be warned, some animals are red to show they taste bad or are even poisonous!

Spot the difference

Can you find two differences between these wiggly milk snakes?

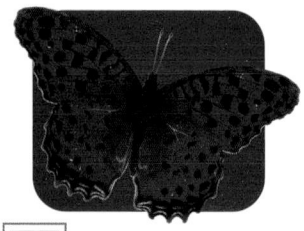

WATCH OUT!

The ladybug has a cunning trick. It oozes a nasty-tasting goo from its knees! The red color warns other animals that it tastes bad.

What comes next?

Look at the animal patterns. Can you work out which red animal comes next on each line?

Use your stickers here!

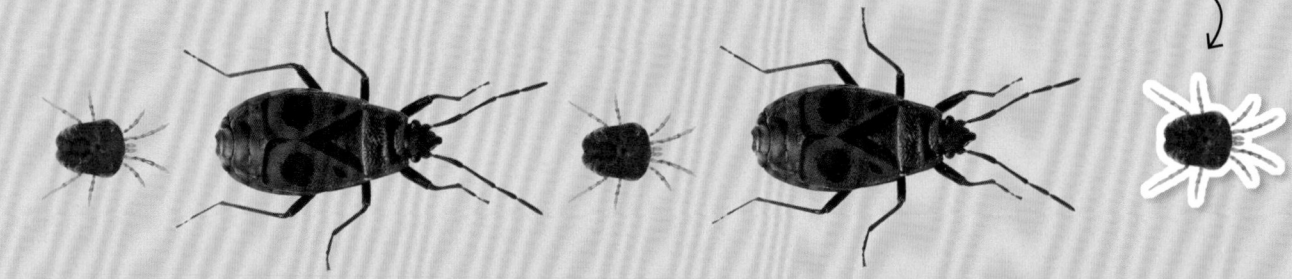

Draw the other half

Copy the patterns to complete the butterflies.

Color me in

Use different shades of red to color in the striped fish.

Which has the most spots?

One of these ladybugs has more spots than the others. Can you spot it?

LOOK AT ME!

The male frigate bird puffs out its bright red chest to attract a mate.

Who likes shrimp?

Follow the lines to find out which bird eats shrimp.

Strawberry finch

Scarlet ibis

Red cardinal

Shrimp

Cherries

Sticker scene

How many red crabs can you find on your sticker sheet? Fill the beach with red crabs!

Use your stickers here!

Orange

Orange animals, such as Monarch butterflies, are easy to spot. But their bright color sends a message to hungry birds. It tells them to stay away—these butterflies are horrible to eat.

Cat
Sea stars
Corn snake
Gila monster
Sea slug
Sea urchin
Grasshoppers
Orangutan
Newts
Tomato frog
Slug
Crab
Clownfish

Caterpillar
Monarch butterflies
Llama
Stag beetle
Atlas moth
Cock-of-the-rock
Tiger
Butterflies
Pigeon blood discus fish
Kitten
Bearded dragon
Tarantula
Hummingbird
Scorpion
Parakeets
Goldfish

Scarlet minivet
Macaws
Silk moth
Owl
Butterfly
Giant firefly
Box turtle
Piglets
Ants
Bat
Telescope goldfish
Discus fish
Hamster
Octopus
Sika deer

Tiger
Toucan
Discus fish
Cat
Rabbit
Tree frogs
Monarch butterflies
Tomato frog
Red crab
French bulldog
Blue-winged pitta
Killifish
Dhole
Tree frog
Sika deer
Pufferfish
Tarantula
Clownfish

Fiery orange

Close your eyes and think of three different orange animals. They could be furry or scaly, big, or small. Are they on this page?

Mini-beast mix up!

Can you find four ants, three butterflies, two caterpillars, and one cricket?

FLOWER POWER

The African queen butterfly is a tasty snack for a bird. The orange butterfly sits on an orange flower to hide, or camouflage.

Word search

These orange animals are all in the word grid. Can you find them?

c	a	t	m	t
k	n	g	w	i
c	t	o	n	g
m	o	t	h	e
s	d	e	e	r

Moth

Deer

Ant

Tiger

Cat

Maze

The orange kitten is searching for its favorite toy. Can you help it find its way?

Matching pairs

Look carefully. Can you find two newts that are exactly the same?

Odd one out

Look at the shoal of orange clown fish. Which one doesn't match the others?

HIDDEN TIGER

A tiger's orange stripes help it to hide in the grass. The tiger hides so it can creep up on the animal it hunts.

Follow the lines

The orangutans are very hungry. Which one will reach its favorite fruit?

How many left?

Each flower can only have one butterfly land on it. How many butterflies will need to keep fluttering?

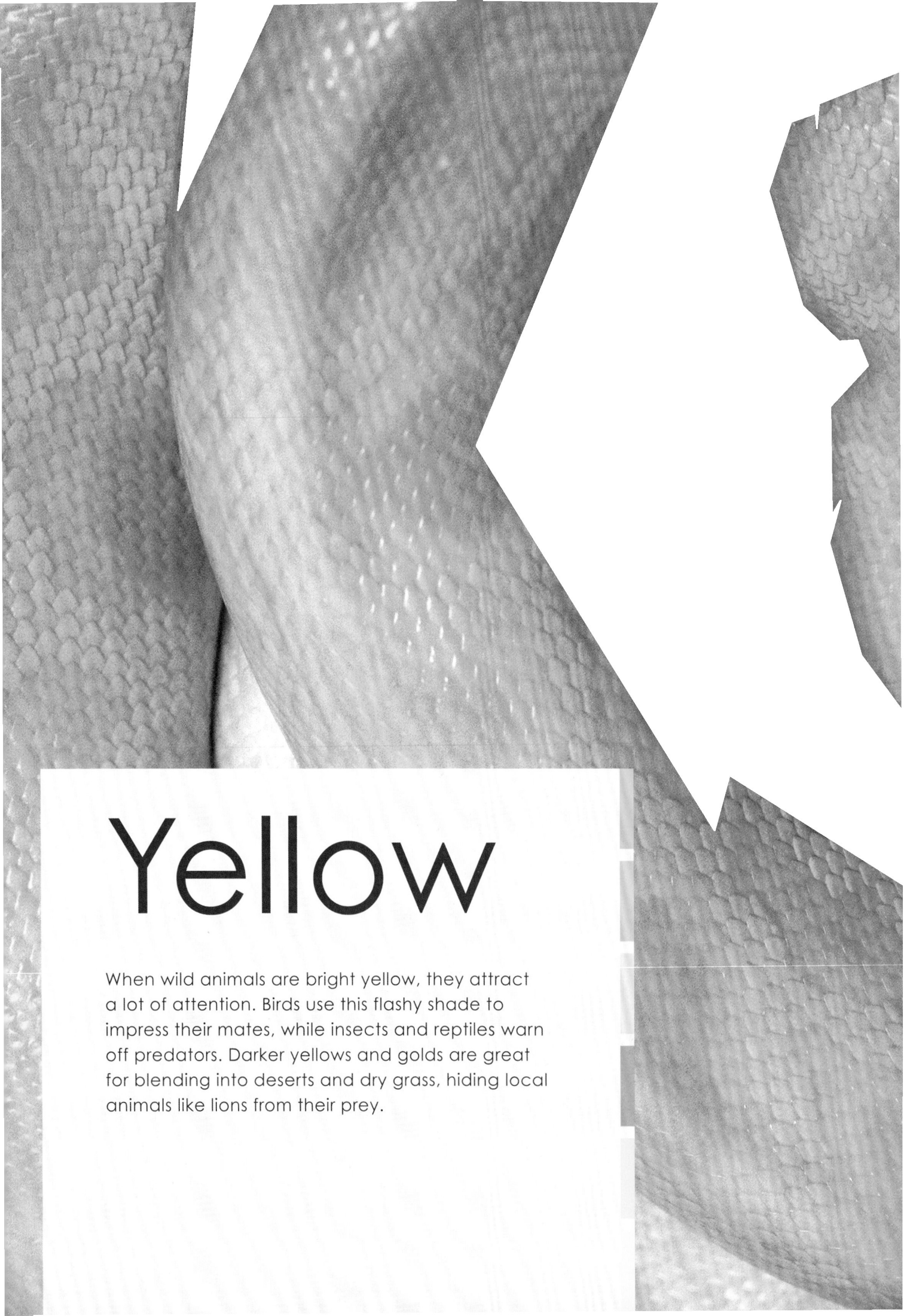

Yellow

When wild animals are bright yellow, they attract a lot of attention. Birds use this flashy shade to impress their mates, while insects and reptiles warn off predators. Darker yellows and golds are great for blending into deserts and dry grass, hiding local animals like lions from their prey.

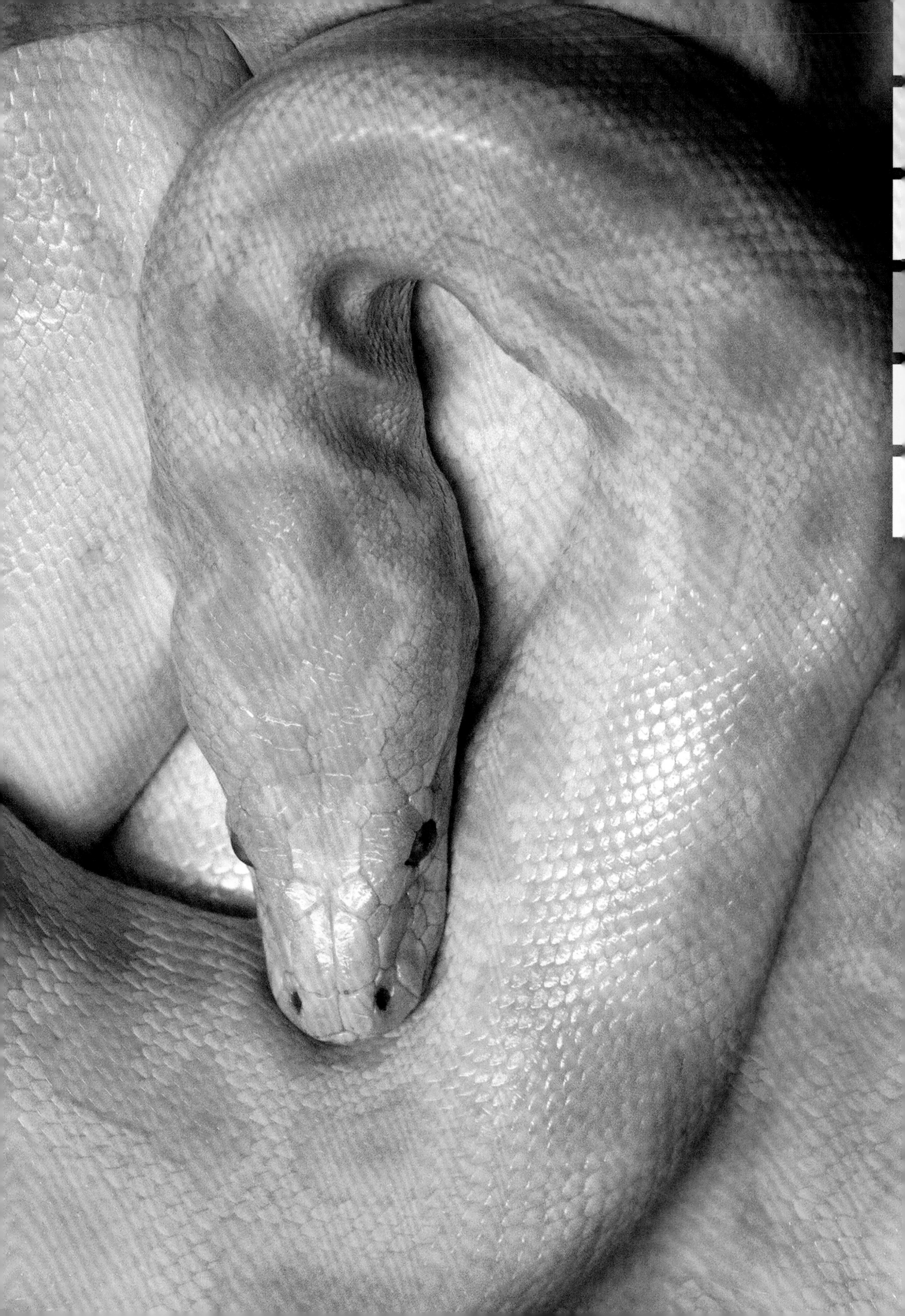

Parakeets
Seahorses
Chicks
Fire salamander
Viper
Yellow weevils
Tree frogs
Crab spider
Banana slug
Bearded dragon
Python
Brain sponge
Yellow tang
Trevally fish
Butterflyfish

Land crab
Coal tit
Weaver bird
Orange tip butterflies
Box fish
Wasps
Cane toads
Snails
Lion cub
Golden poison frog
Leopard gecko
Gold ram fish

Canary
Monarch butterflies
Sunbird
Butterfly
Trumpet snails
Corn snakes
Ladybugs
Yellow tang
Cheetah
Butterflies
Ducklings
Macaw
Emperor penguins
Parakeet

Sun parakeet
Crabs
Butterflies
Sea anemone
Tree frog
Grove snails
Python
Lion
Foxface rabbitfish
Axolotl
Labrador retriever puppy
Butterflies

Sunny yellow

How many yellow animals can you see on these pages? You'll need to unscramble, spot, and search to solve the puzzles.

Help the buzzing bee

The bee wants to buzz to the biggest yellow flower. Which path should it choose?

DEADLY YELLOW

The golden poison dart frog is one of the most poisonous animals in the world. Its yellow color warns "don't eat me!"

Find the shadows

The yellow animals have lost their shadows!
Can you find them?

Dot to dot

Connect the dots, starting at number 1. Which super-slow, yellow animal will appear?

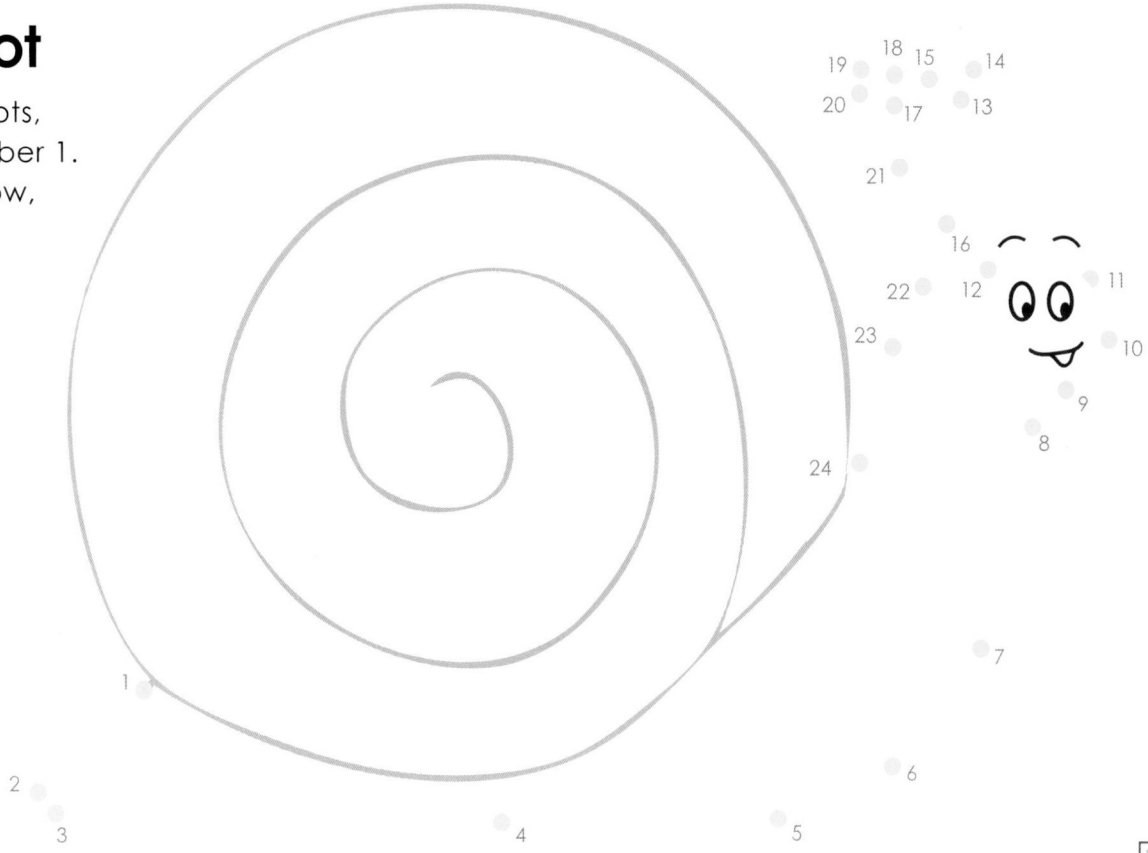

Maze

The duck is trying to find its lost duckling. Can you help?

start

finish

Odd one out

Look carefully at the golden beetles. Which one doesn't match the others?

COLOR CHANGE

This yellow seahorse has a neat trick. It can make its skin darker to hide among sea plants.

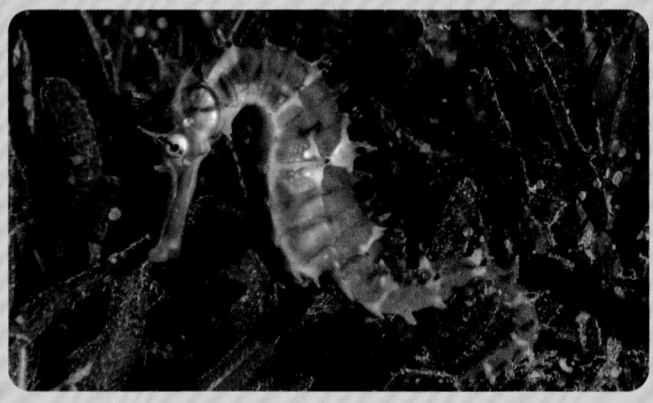

Draw the other half

Draw and color in the other half of the crab.

Word search

Can you find the yellow animals in the word grid?

t	c	u	b	s
f	i	s	h	n
r	d	l	l	a
o	m	u	n	i
g	t	g	f	l

Fish

Slug

Snail

Frog

Cub

Green

For hiding among leaves and undergrowth, green is the perfect disguise. It allows this little lizard to sneak up on juicy insects to eat. The insects don't see the lizard until it is too late.

Leaf mimic katydid
Scarab beetle
Damselfish
Gecko
Red-eyed tree frog
Butterfly
Grasshopper
Swallowtail caterpillar
Eastern green mamba
Shining pot beetles
Crocodile
Parrotfish
Egyptian green toad
Tree frog
Butterfly
Butterfly
Terrapin
Bearded dragon
Flower beetle
Caterpillar
Mantis
Arboreal lizard
Lanternfly
Praying mantis
Green parrot
Parakeet

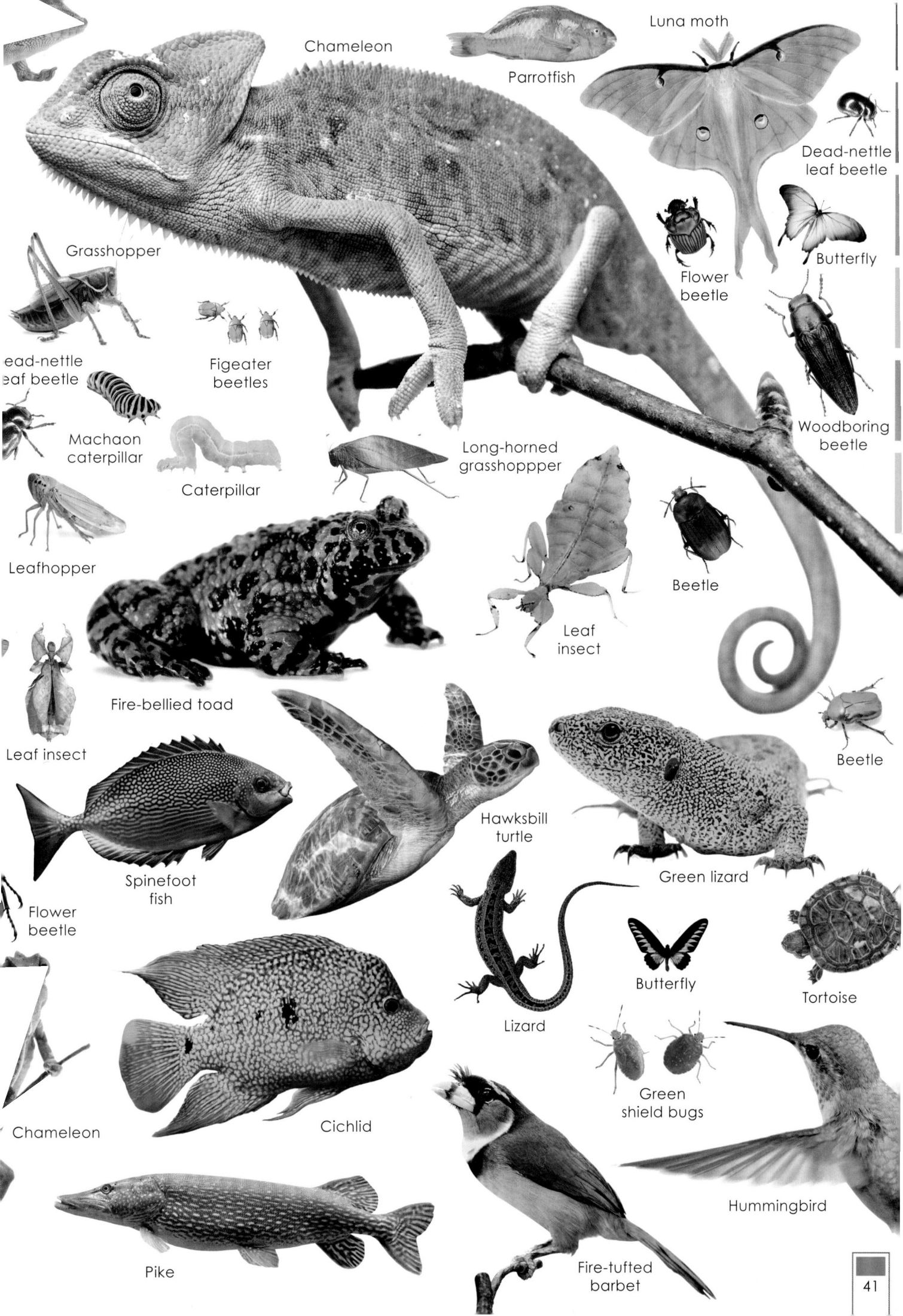
Chameleon
Parrotfish
Luna moth
Dead-nettle leaf beetle
Grasshopper
Flower beetle
Butterfly
ead-nettle
eaf beetle
Figeater beetles
Woodboring beetle
Machaon caterpillar
Caterpillar
Long-horned grasshoppper
Leafhopper
Beetle
Leaf insect
Fire-bellied toad
Leaf insect
Beetle
Hawksbill turtle
Spinefoot fish
Green lizard
Flower beetle
Butterfly
Tortoise
Lizard
Green shield bugs
Chameleon
Cichlid
Hummingbird
Pike
Fire-tufted barbet

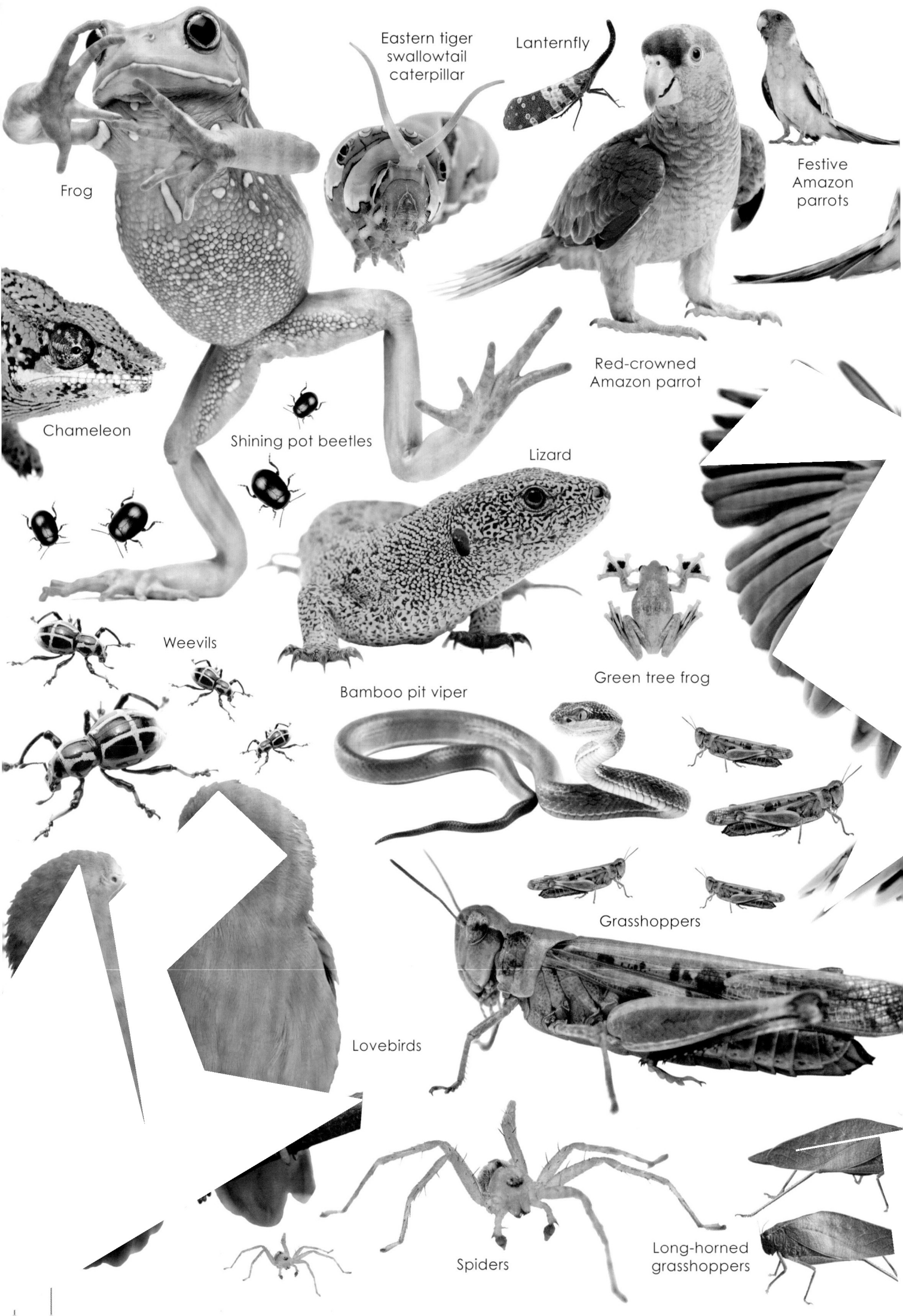
Eastern tiger swallowtail caterpillar
Lanternfly
Frog
Festive Amazon parrots
Red-crowned Amazon parrot
Chameleon
Shining pot beetles
Lizard
Weevils
Green tree frog
Bamboo pit viper
Grasshoppers
Lovebirds
Spiders
Long-horned grasshoppers

Alexandrine parakeet
Weevils
Asterope sapphira butterfly
Sunset moth
Fire-tufted barbet
Red-eyed tree frog
Iguana
Figeater beetles
Plumed basilisk
Red-eyed tree frog
Amazon parrot
Green tree frog
Australian green tree frog
Rabbitfish
Red-eyed tree frog
Blue-green chromis
Lanternflies
Iguana
Monkey grasshopper

Going green

Green is a useful color when you need to hide in the forest. How many green insects, birds, and lizards can you find hiding in these tricky puzzles?

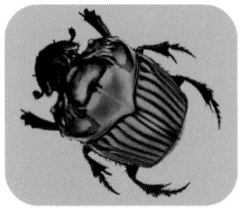

Spot the difference

Can you find the three differences between these two caterpillars?

GREEN FUR

This sloth looks green because of algae growing on its fur. It helps the sloth to hide from predators.

Matching pair

Find the two identical beetles below.

Color me in

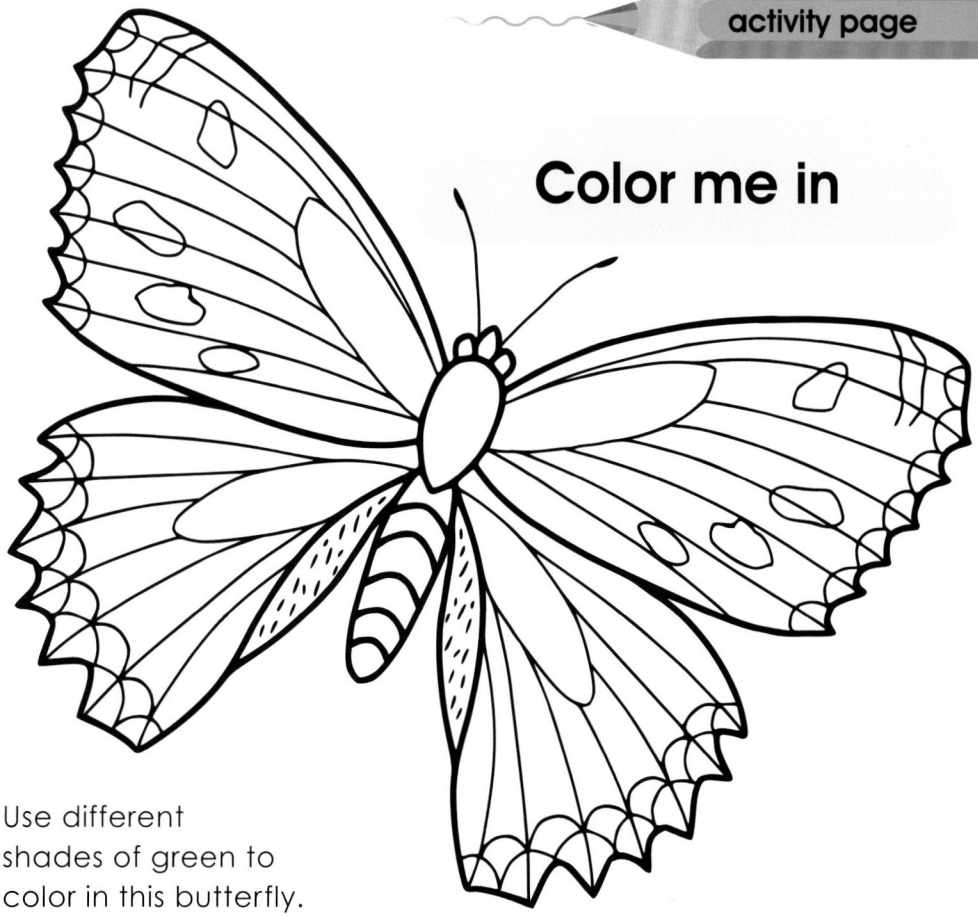

Use different shades of green to color in this butterfly.

What comes next?

Look at the patterns below and work out which green creature comes next.

Use your stickers here!

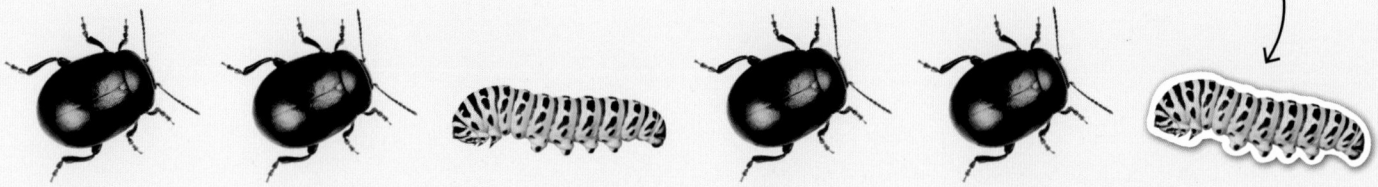

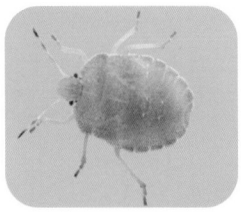

Find the cricket!

The red-eyed tree frogs all want to reach the delicious cricket. Which one gets the tasty snack?

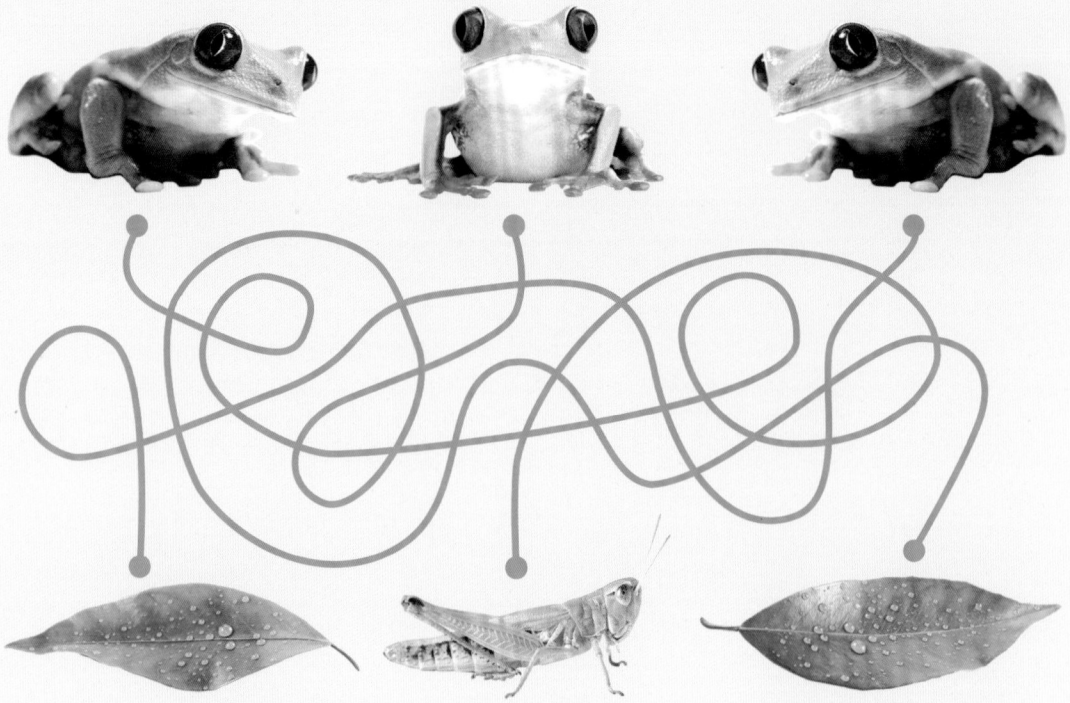

Which one has the most?

The parrots have found some crunchy nuts. Which one has the most?

WAIT AND HIDE

The green tree snake hides among the leaves. It keeps still and waits for an animal it wants to eat to pass. Then it pounces!

What's missing?

One of the luna moths is missing a spot. Can you spot which one?

Snake snack

The snake is looking for its dinner. Look at the shadow. Can you see which animal it has found?

Blue

Blue is a color used for showing off on land, but in the sea it is used for blending in. The fish in this huge shoal match the blue of the water, making them difficult to count. Their enemies, such as sharks, find it tricky to pick them out to catch and eat.

Blue tits
Blue crayfish
Longhorn beetle
Dart frog
Violet ground beetle
Macaw
Blue-crested lizard
Woodboring beetles
Leaf beetles
Violet ground beetles
beetle
Weevil beetles
Blue discus fish
Betta fish
Blue spotted fish
Powder blue tang fish
Victoria crowned pigeon

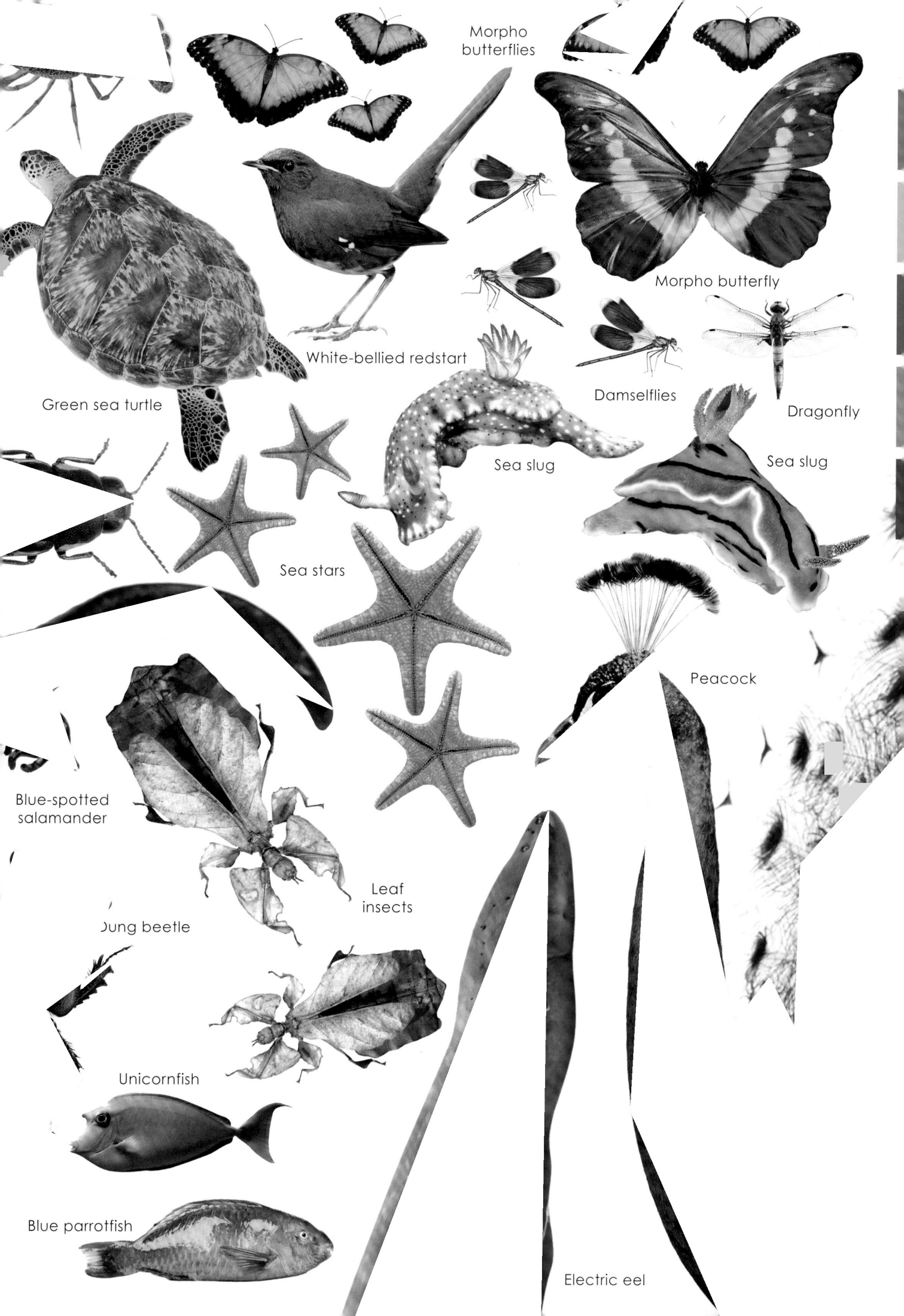
Morpho butterflies
Morpho butterfly
White-bellied redstart
Green sea turtle
Damselflies
Dragonfly
Sea slug
Sea slug
Sea stars
Peacock
Blue-spotted salamander
Leaf insects
Dung beetle
Unicornfish
Blue parrotfish
Electric eel

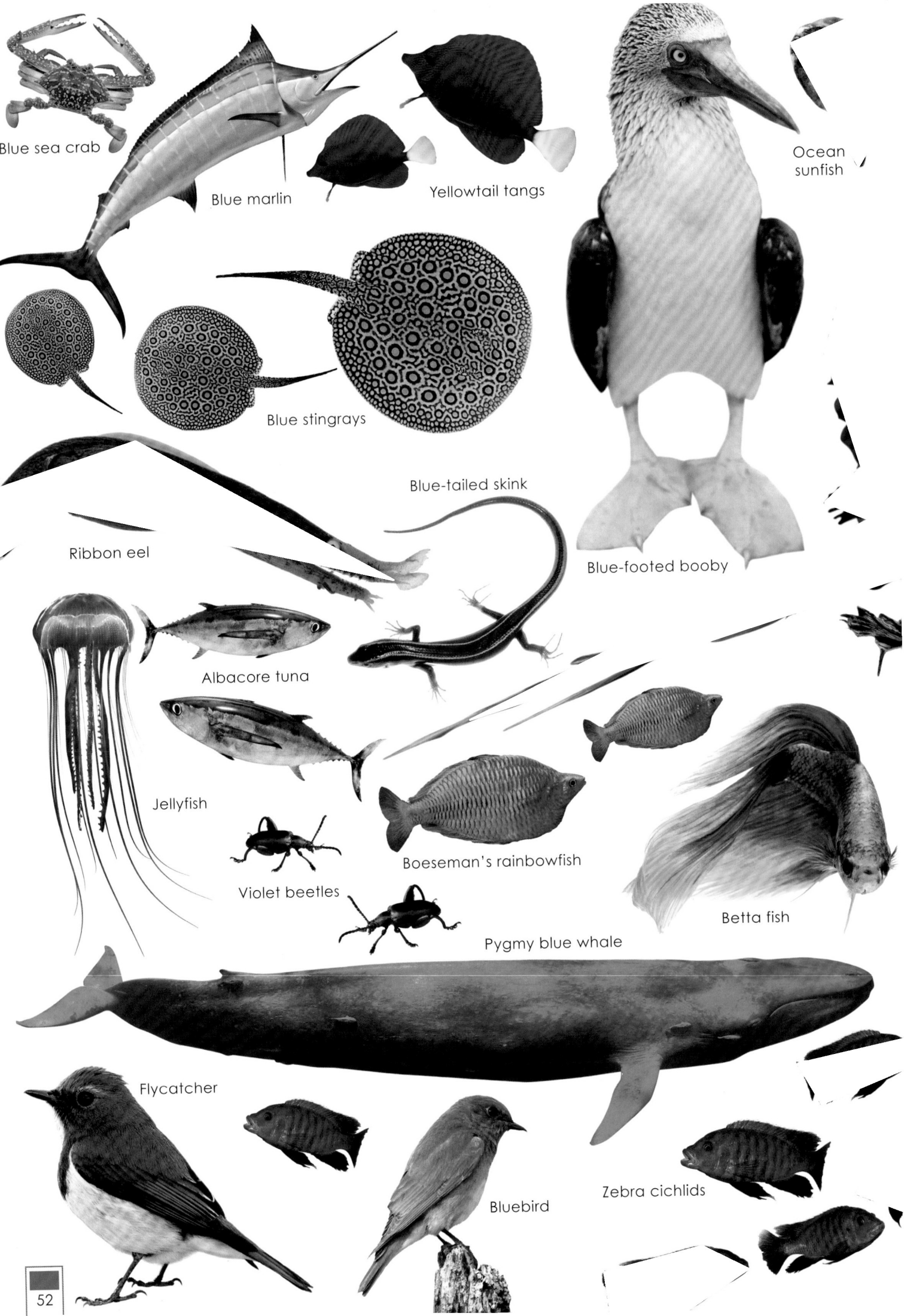
Blue sea crab
Blue marlin
Yellowtail tangs
Ocean sunfish
Blue stingrays
Blue-tailed skink
Ribbon eel
Blue-footed booby
Albacore tuna
Jellyfish
Violet beetles
Boeseman's rainbowfish
Betta fish
Pygmy blue whale
Flycatcher
Bluebird
Zebra cichlids

Common blue butterflies
Bluebird
Masked lovebird
Sea slug
Macaw
Blue lobster
Betta fish
Damselfly
Boxfish
Parrotfish
Betta fish
Betta fish
Black-crowned
night heron
Parrotfish

Bright blue

Dive in to these puzzles to find out which blue creatures live underwater, which live on land, and which fly high in the skies.

Sticker scene

Find the matching parrot fish sticker on your sheet, and add it to the coral scene. Can you find any more blue fish?

Use your stickers here!

BLUE FOOT

The male blue-footed booby dances on its blue feet to attract a mate. The brighter the blue, the more impressed a female will be!

How many left?

Each water lilly can only have one dragonfly land on it. How many dragonflies won't be able to land?

Rescue the chicks!

The blue jay is trying to get back to its nest. Can you help it?

start

finish

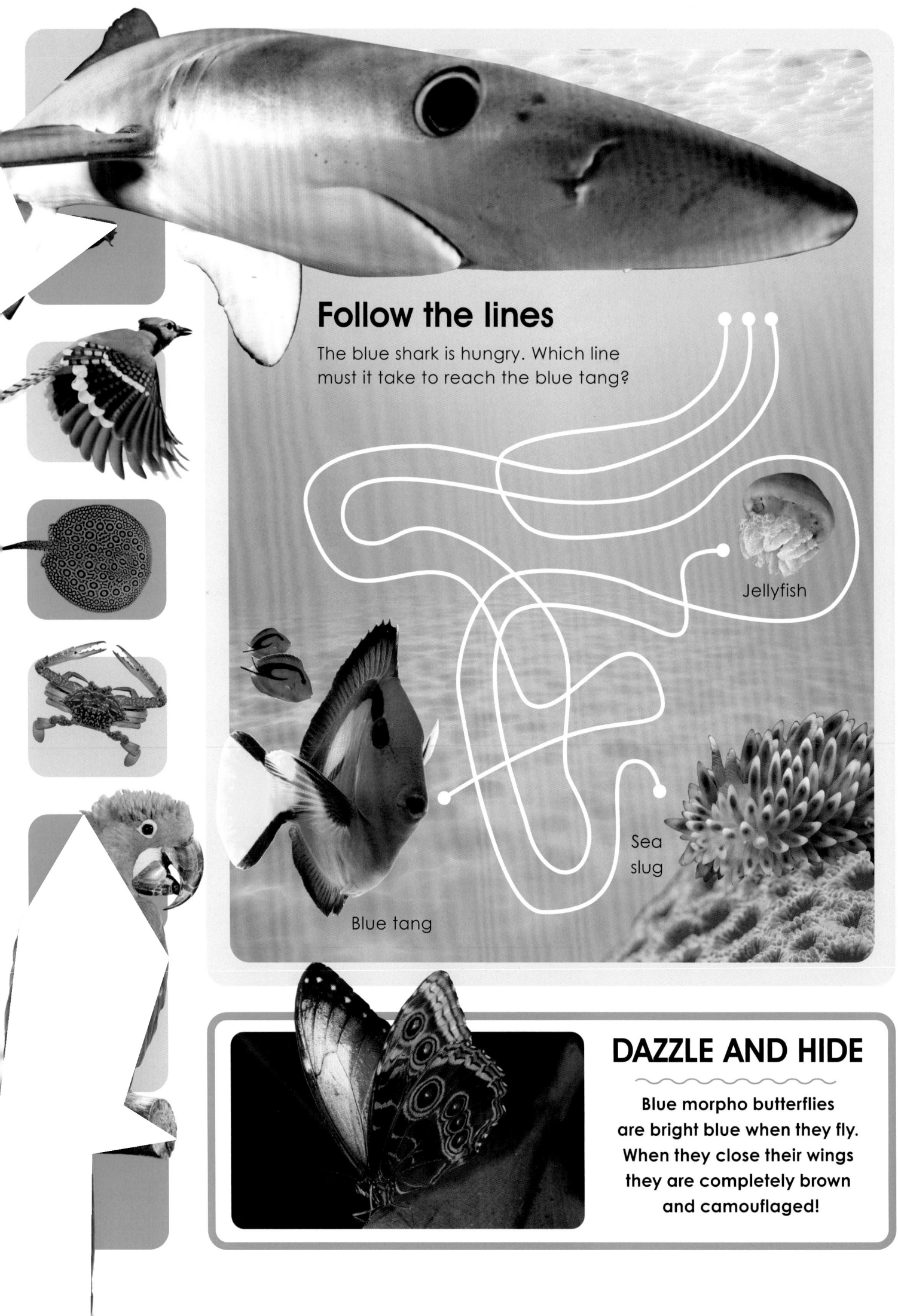
Follow the lines
The blue shark is hungry. Which line must it take to reach the blue tang?
Jellyfish
Sea slug
Blue tang
DAZZLE AND HIDE
Blue morpho butterflies are bright blue when they fly. When they close their wings they are completely brown and camouflaged!

Odd one out

There is one beetle that is different. Can you spot it?

Draw the other half

Can you draw the other half of the flying parrot?

Match the shadows

Match the blue animals to their shadows.

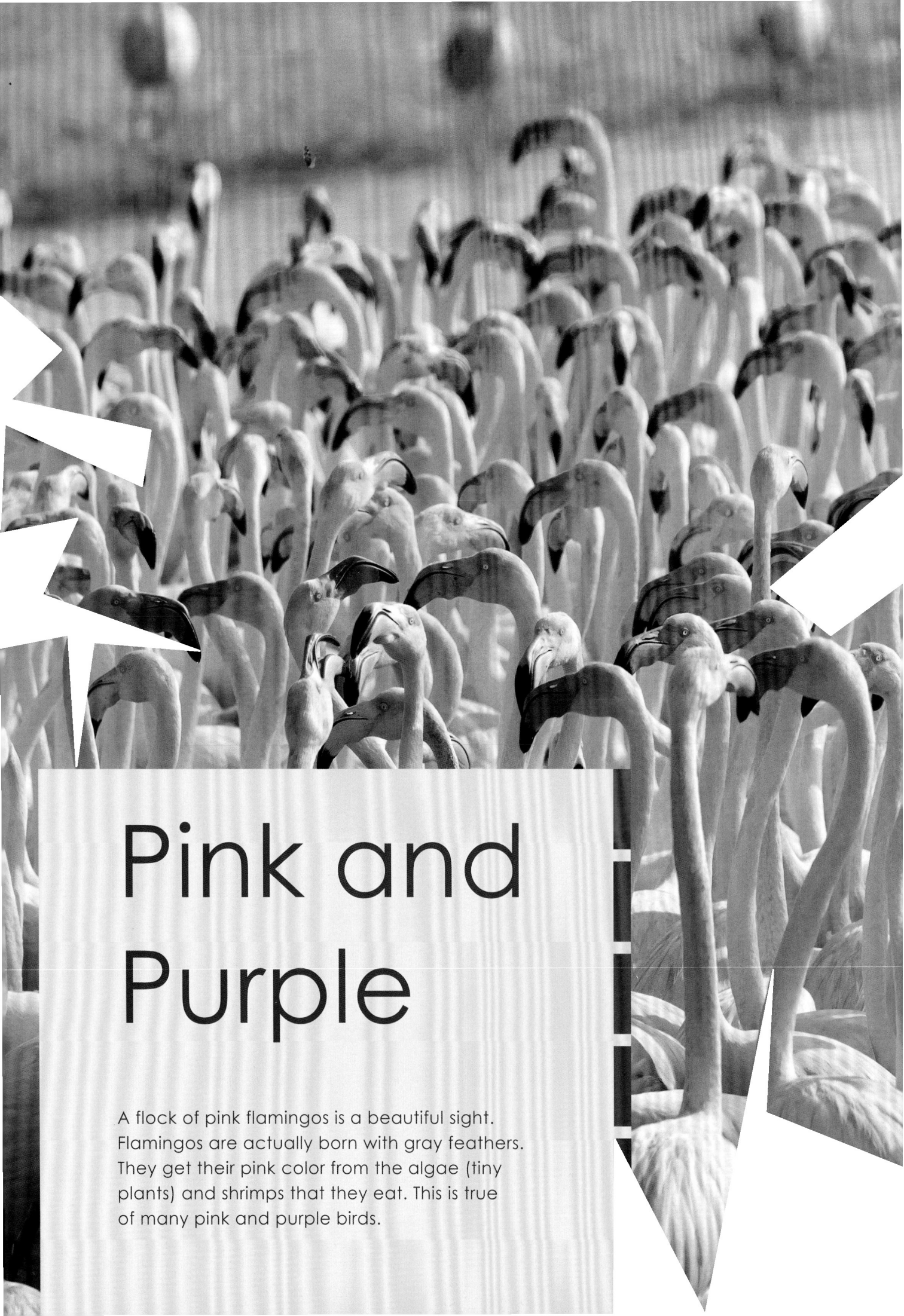

Pink and Purple

A flock of pink flamingos is a beautiful sight. Flamingos are actually born with gray feathers. They get their pink color from the algae (tiny plants) and shrimps that they eat. This is true of many pink and purple birds.

Pink butterflies
Phasmatodea
Roseate spoonbill
Pink butterflies
Elephant hawk-moth
Sphynx cat
Sea stars
Anthias
Pygmy seahorse
Orchid mantis
Japanese macaque
Sawfly larva
Flamingo
Flamingo
Sea mollusk
Pig
Scallop

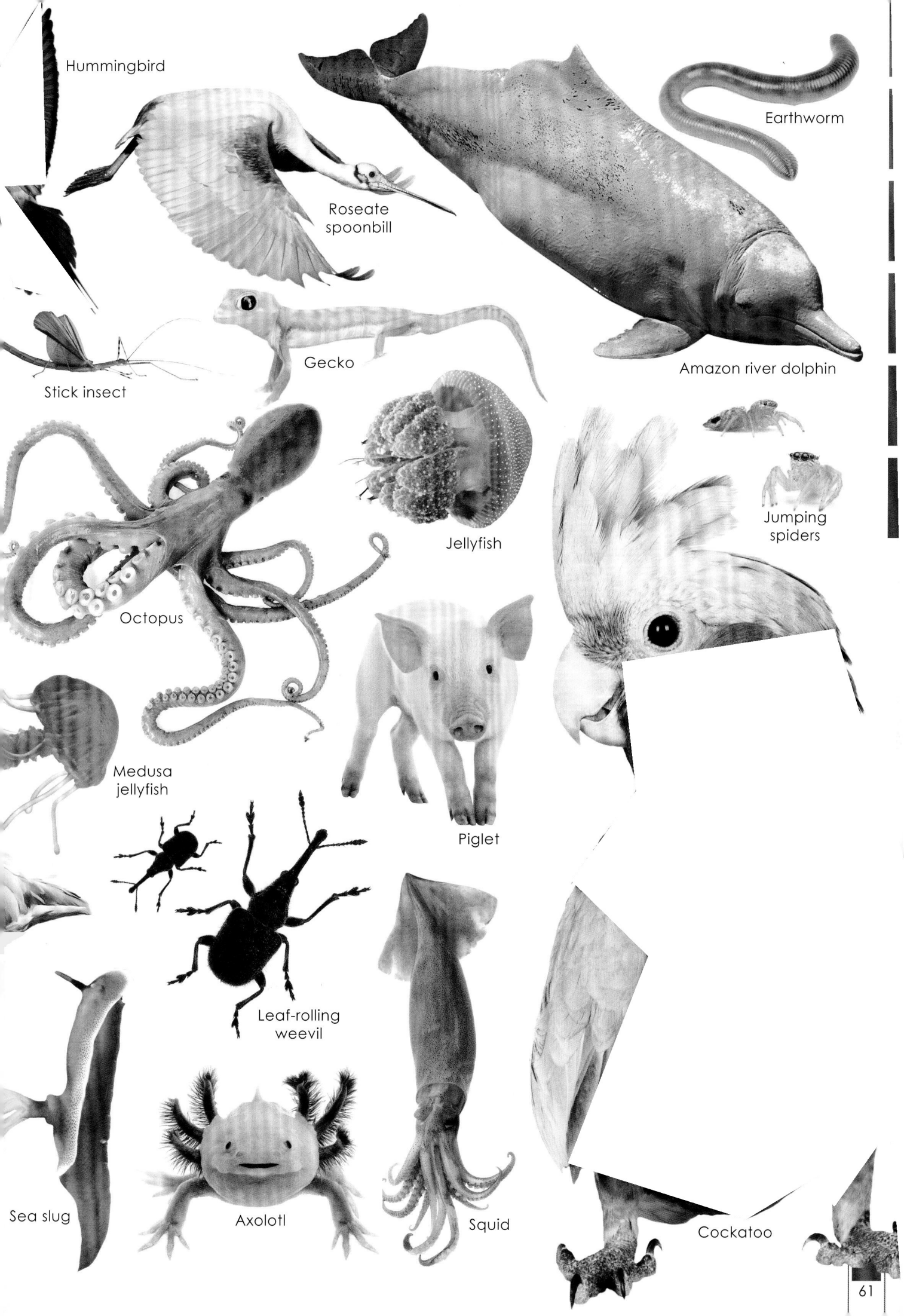
Hummingbird
Roseate spoonbill
Earthworm
Amazon river dolphin
Gecko
Stick insect
Jellyfish
Jumping spiders
Octopus
Medusa jellyfish
Piglet
Leaf-rolling weevil
Sea slug
Axolotl
Squid
Cockatoo

Pink puzzles

There are lots of flying pink creatures in these pretty pink puzzles. Find the answers before they flutter away.

Matching pair

Look at the fluttering butterflies. Can you find two that are the same?

ALL CHANGE

Baby flamingos are white when they are born. The food they eat makes their feathers pink!

Color me in

Use different shades of pink to color in this hummingbird.

What comes next?

Look at the order of the animals and work out which comes next.

Use your stickers here!

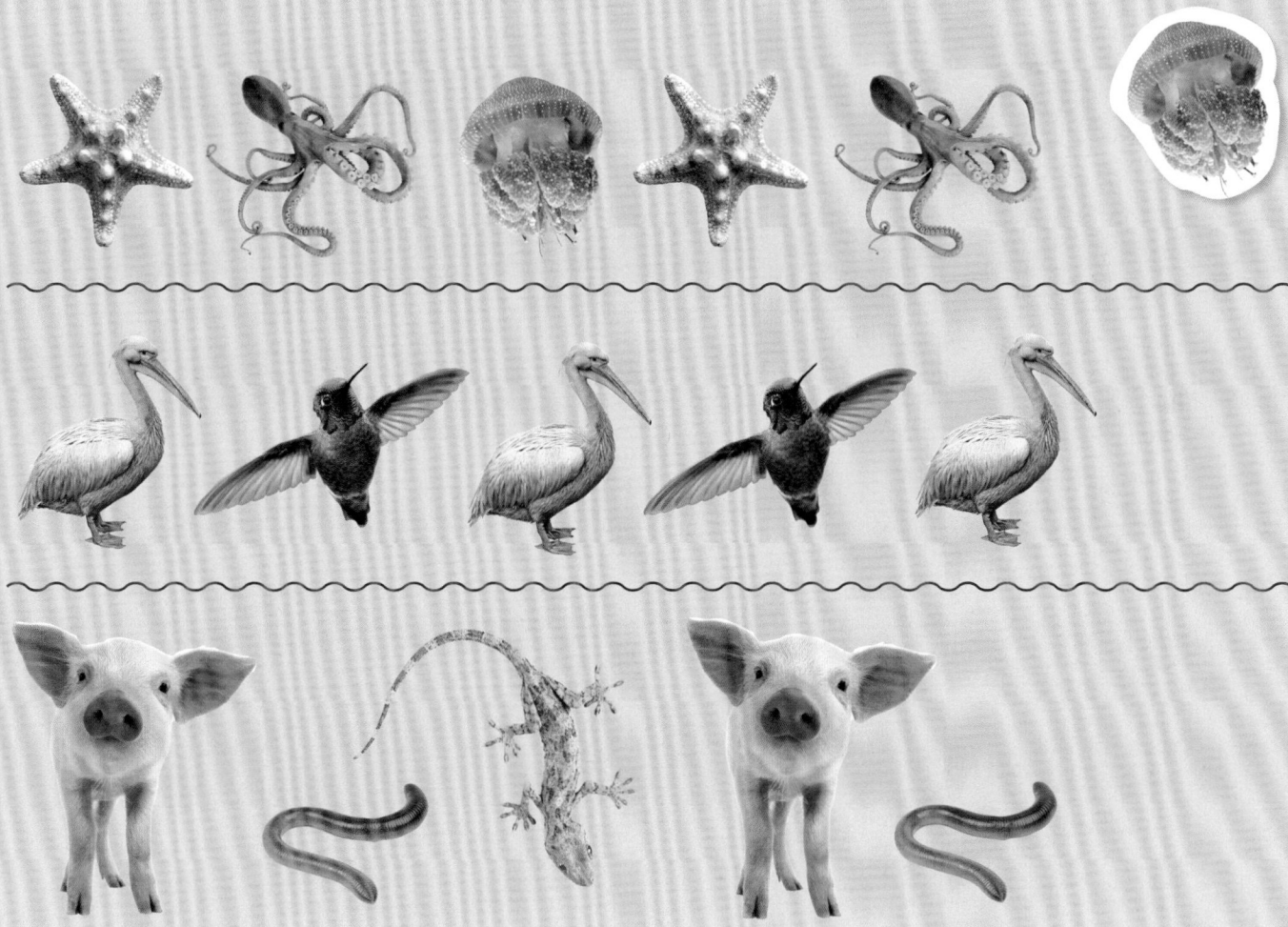

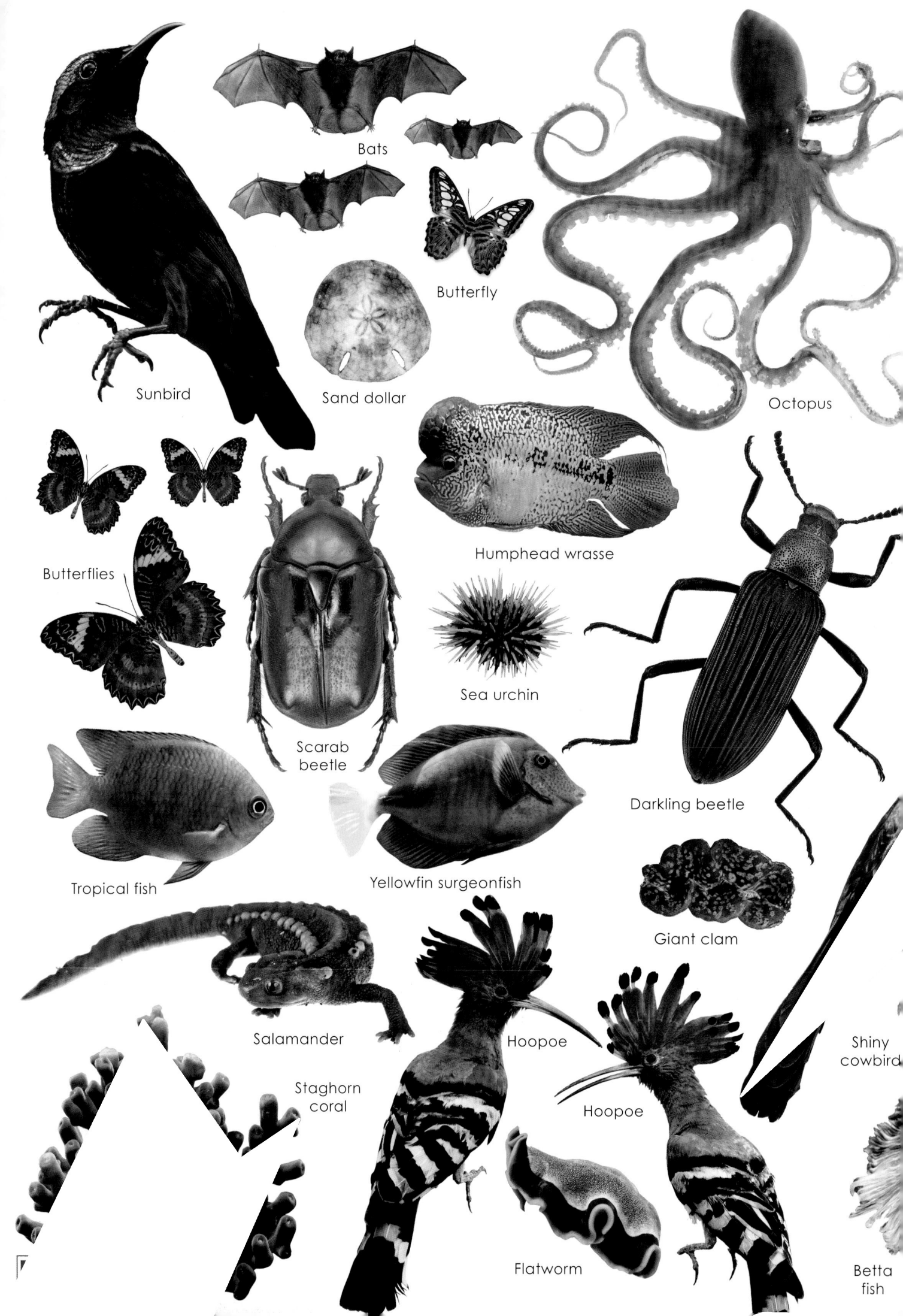
Bats
Butterfly
Sunbird
Sand dollar
Octopus
Butterflies
Humphead wrasse
Sea urchin
Scarab beetle
Darkling beetle
Tropical fish
Yellowfin surgeonfish
Giant clam
Salamander
Hoopoe
Shiny cowbird
Staghorn coral
Hoopoe
Flatworm
Betta fish

Sea stars
Poison dart frogs
Butterflies
Violet sea snail
Sea slug
Parrotfish
Tropical fish
Tropical fish
Hummingbird
Sea urchins
Scarab beetle
Brush-footed butterfly
Orchid mantis
Flatworm
Macaw
Butterflies
Blue tangs
Hummingbird
Dragonfly
Spanish shawl sea slug

Purple patch

Do you love the color purple? What is your favorite purple animal? Can you see it on this page?

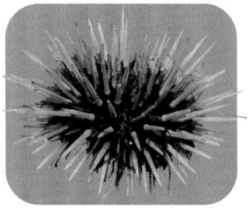

Sticker scene

The purple butterfly loves these purple flowers. How many more purple butterflies can you find on your sticker sheet to add to the scene?

Use your stickers here!

ROYAL PURPLE

Bow down to the purple emperor butterfly! It got its name because purple is a royal color for emperors, kings, and queens.

Word search

Can you find these purple creatures in the letter grid?

m	f	i	s	h
a	r	m	t	s
c	o	r	a	l
a	g	v	e	p
w	c	l	a	m

Fish

Clam

Macaw

Coral

Frog

Ocean commotion

Only one of these creatures will find the coral. Which one is it?

Starfish

Sea urchin

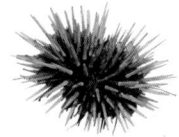

Sea urchin

Yellowfin surgeonfish

Sea slug

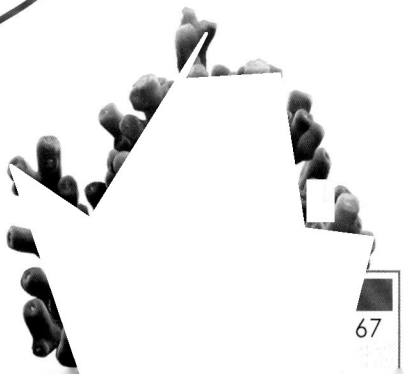

Coral

Brown

Animals that live in woods, deserts, or on the ground are often brown to blend in. It's tricky to spot the brown insects rushing around among these dead twigs and leaves.

Praying mantis
Silkmoth
Pheasant
Eagle owl
Bactrian camel
Wolf spider
Snail
Toad
Leafwing butterfly
Hedgehog
Katydid
Greenbottle blue tarantula
Duck
Stick insect
Redknee tarantula
Red deer
Grasshopper
Song thrush
Mantis
Owl
Russian tortoise
Stag beetle
Rhinoceros beetle
Caterpillar
Crested gecko
Red squirrel
Amazon tree boa
Diadem butterfly

Rabbit
Box turtle
Scorpion
Cricket
Pheasants
Grapevine beetle
Brown bear
Amazonian bush cricket
Moorish gecko
Millipede
Meerkat
Leaf insect
Giraffe
Turkestan cockroach
Longhorn beetle
Bush cricket
Butterfly
Mole cricket
Joey
Red angaroo
Hedgehog
Cricket

Arab mare and colt
California sea lion
Rabbit
Red kangaroo
Stink bug
Gelbvieh bull
Llamas
Red setter
Eagle owl
Penguin chick
Steppe eagle
Grizzly bear
Red panda
Darkling beetle
Chafer beetle
Caracals
Stag beetle
Alpacas
White-tailed deer

Shetland pony
Fruit bat
Chow chow
Trout
Cricket
Shield bug
Orb-weaver spider
Goat
Moth
Indian black antelope
Moth caterpillar
Leaf mimic katydid
Silkmoth
Cat
Viper
Ants
Wild boar piglet
Moorish gecko
Grapevine beetle
Centipedes
Sonoran desert toad
Snail
Orangutan

Brown is the perfect color to hide against the ground or in trees. Can you hunt out the camouflaged animals in these puzzles?

Dot to dot

What is slowly walking across this page? Connect the dots to find out.

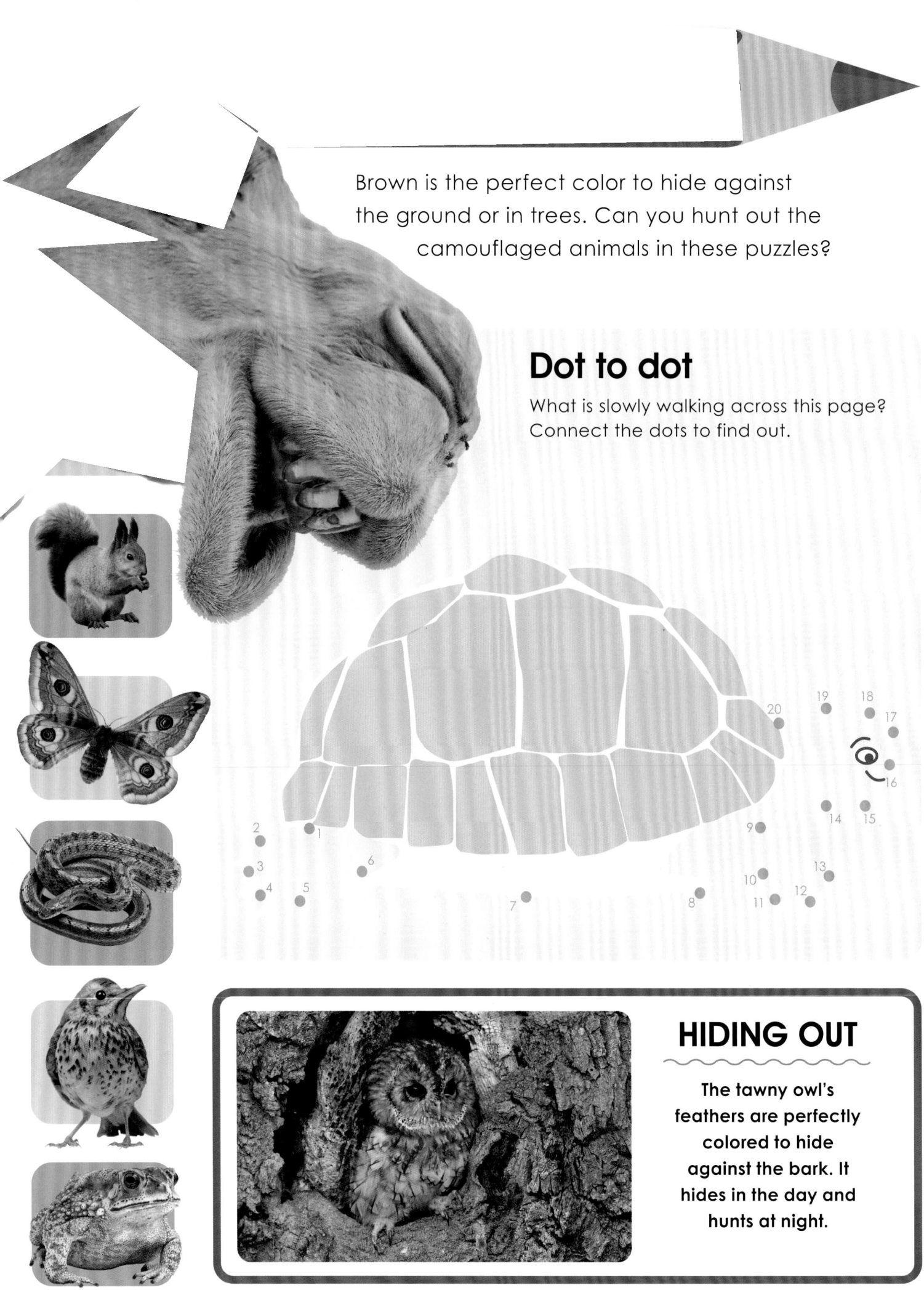

HIDING OUT

The tawny owl's feathers are perfectly colored to hide against the bark. It hides in the day and hunts at night.

Find the matching pair

Can you find two spiky hedgehogs that are exactly the same?

Shadow search

Look at the shapes carefully. Match each animal to its shadow.

Spot the difference

Can you spot three differences between these giraffes?

Black, White, and Gray

Zebras have stunning black-and-white coats. Their striking colors help to put off flies. It seems that the biting, blood-sucking flies don't like landing on the dazzling stripes. These stripes also confuse predators, by making it hard for them to see individual zebras within the herd.

Aquatic salamander
Scarab beetle
Grass snake
Horse
Scorpion
Butterfly
Tasmanian devil
Flower beetle
Angelfish
Transvaal girdled lizard
Dolphin
Labrador retriever
Giant anteater
Oil beetle
Southern ground hornbill
Black wildebeest
Fire-bellied newt
Egyptian cobra

Great mormon butterfly
Telescope goldfish
Rock monitor lizard
Indian bison
Mole
Sea urchin
Butterfly
Ant
Stag beetle
Red-tailed black shark
Skate
Minotaur beetle
Cat
Chimpanzee
Dog
Bess beetle
Angelfish
Armored beetles
Clownfish

American bison
Curlyhair tarantula
Giant snakehead fish
Ferret
Leopard
Alpine newt
Peacock moth
Rhinoceros beetle
Leaf beetle
Butterfly
Minks
Italian mastiff
Black moor goldfish
Giant Panda
Curlyhair tarantulas
Humboldt penguins
Sea lion pup

Black widow spider
Rook
Jackdaw
Bonobo
Bald eagle
Rook
Horned beetle
Rooster
Gorilla
Magpie
Griffon vulture
Ferret
Orca whale
Sturgeon
Carpet beetle
Llama
Pot-bellied piglet
Earless seal
Stag beetle

Black

A black animal is perfectly hidden at night. How many black animals can you find in these puzzles?

Word search

Find the black creatures hiding in this word grid.

d	o	g	s	h
c	p	l	e	o
f	b	e	a	r
d	x	w	l	s
s	n	a	k	e

Snake

Horse

Bear

Dog

Seal

DARK LEOPARD

A panther is actually a leopard! Its spots are so dark that you can't see them well. It hunts at night so it is completely hidden.

What comes next?

Can you work out which animal comes next on each line?
You will find them on your sticker sheet.

Use your stickers here!

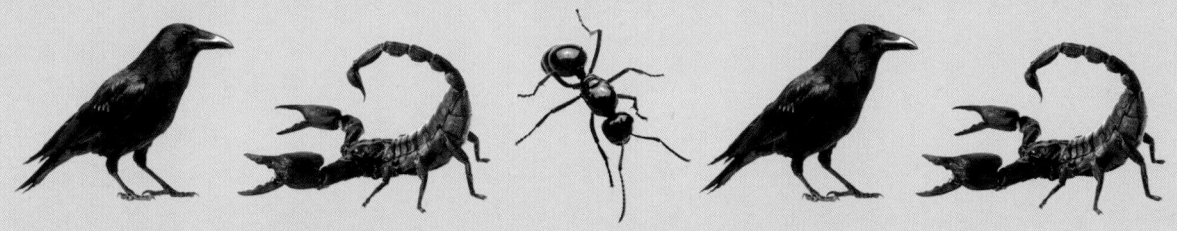

Panda puzzle

The panda is hungry.
Help it to find the bamboo leaves it loves to eat.

Tamandua
Pyrenean mountain dog
Rat
Humboldt penguin
Alaskan malamute puppy
Butterfly
Albino American alligator
Cabbage butterflies
Snowy owl
Hamster
Mute swan
English bulldog
Tortoise beetle
Crowned sifaka
Maltese puppy
Goat and kid
Emperor penguin
Albino deer
Betta fish
Ermine
Bigeye fish
White lion
Fly larvae
Albino kangaroos
Hedgehog

Turkey
Cow
Caribou
Butterfly
Rat
Snow leopard
Valais lamb
Flamingo
Stork
Gerbil
Arctic fox
Arctic fox
Coral
Brahman calf
Saiga antelope
Betta fish

Albino ferret
Siamese kitten
Moth
Doves
Parrotfish
Capuchin monkey
Butterfly
Duck
Barn owl
Hedgehog
Albino kingsnake
Guinea pig
Pyrenean mountain dog
Butterfish
Chicken
Albino ball python
Bald eagle
Maltese puppy
Fire goby
Humboldt penguin

Ermine
Jezebel butterflies
Kid
Snow leopard gecko
Green tree frog
Kid
Cockatoo
Fly lavae
Crowned sifaka
Gibbon
Clown knifefish
Persian cat
Rabbit
Humboldt penguin
Striped skunk
Rat
Siberian husky puppy
Sheep
Duck
Cabbage butterfly
California kingsnake
Giant panda cub

White

White can be bright! But if animals live in the snow, white feathers and fur hides them perfectly. Can you solve these white, wintery puzzles?

How many left?

Only five ducks have laid their eggs. How many ducks do not have a nest?

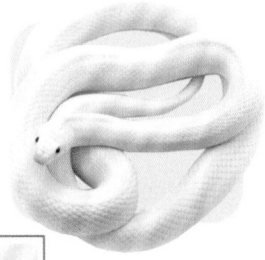

COAT SWAP

The Arctic fox is white in the winter to hide in the snow. In the summer it changes its coat! The fur turns brown to hide it against the ground.

Find the bear twins!

Help the polar bear mom find its two cute cubs.

Matching pair

Only two of the butterflies are the same. Can you spot the matching pair?

Oil beetle
Ant
White-backed vulture
Dove
Buzzard eagle
Sphynx kitten
Rabbit
Goose
Giant anteater
Greater kudu
Owlet
Desert horned lizard
Komodo dragon
Grey crowned crane
Koala
Warthog
Short-nosed unicornfish
Pufferfish
African grey parrot
Tapir

fferfish
Giant anteater
Otter
Scottish fold cat
Sphynx cat
Hippopotamus
Coypu
Weimaraner
Chinchillas
Wolf
Rat
Jackdaw
Seagulls
Macaque monkey
Short-nosed unicornfish
Verreaux's eagle-owl
African pompano
Tinselfish
Cow
British shorthair cat
Foureye butterflyfish

Andalusian horse
Kiwis
Tawny frogmouth
White rhinoceros
Rhinoceros
White-faced owl
Snowy owl
Clymene dolphin
Jackdaw
Aardvark
Pig
Arctic fox
Chinchillas
Cockatiel
Dwarf hamsters
Hawaiian gosling
Herring
Hippopotamus
Pangasius
Bottlenose dolphin
Raccoon
Whale shark
Stingray

Bonnethead shark
Poodle
Alligator hatchling
Cockatiels
Giant anteater
Heron
Rat
Raccoon
Ferret
Lop-eared rabbit
Wombats
African grey parrot
Scottish fold kitten
Kangaroo
Komodo dragon
African elephant
As elept
Rats
Warthog
Florida pompano
Japanese macaques
Silver barb
Tiger shark
Sugar glider
Mole

Multi-colored

Many animals are multi-colored or have striking patterns. This allows them to hide from their enemies by matching patterns of light and shadows in nature, but can also be a way of standing out from the crowd.

Parrot
Chameleon
Chameleon
Red-eyed tree frog
Gupp,
Pink-necked green pigeon
Macaw
Parrotfish
Red-eyed tree frog
Masked lovebirds
Banded pitta
Mandrill
Clown triggerfish
Budgerigar
Peacock
Sea slug
Lorikeet
European bee-eater
Blue-crested lizard
Gouldian finch
Titan triggerfish
Parakeet
Spanish shawl sea slug
Sulawesi hornbill
Dung beetle

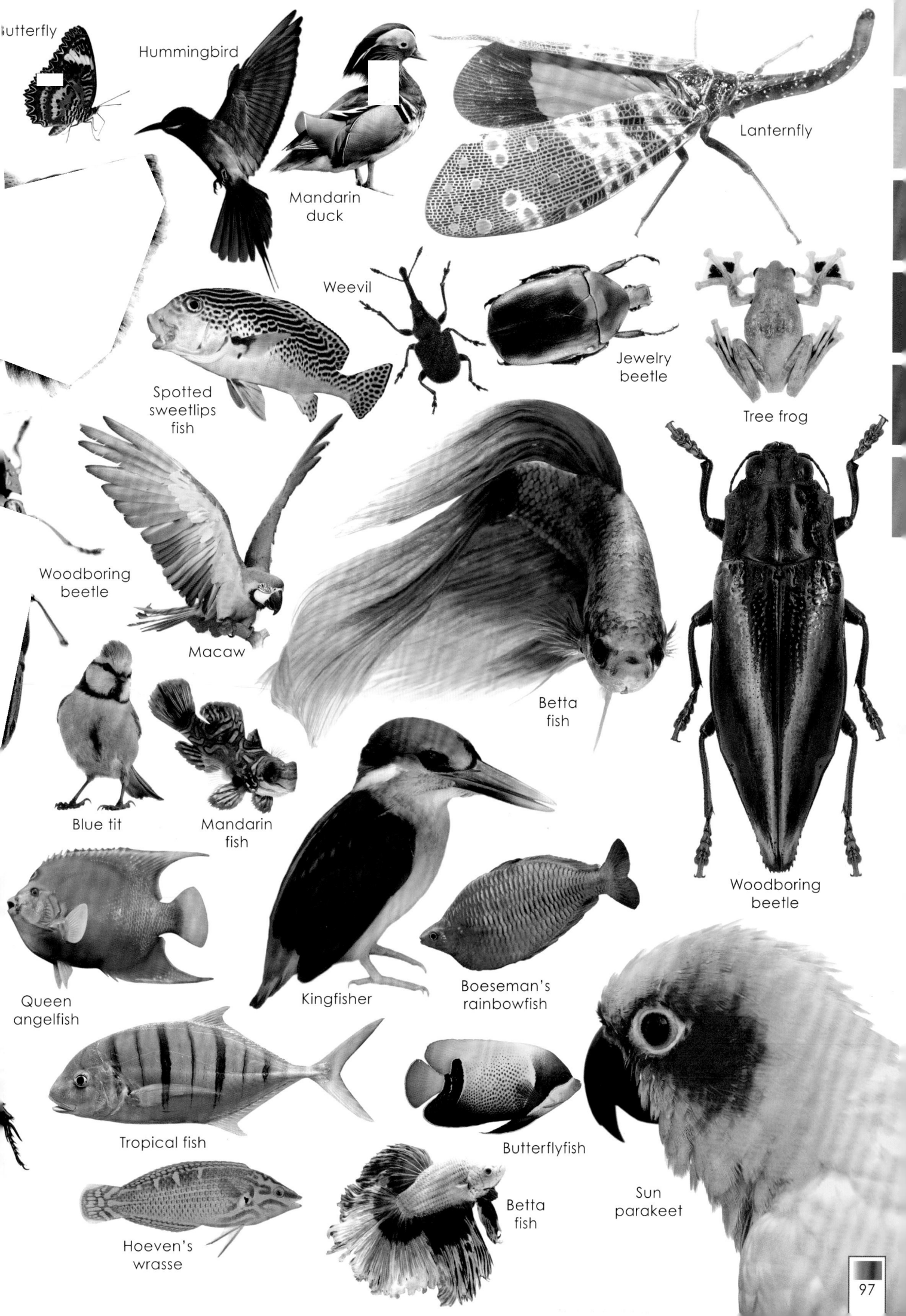
utterfly
Hummingbird
Mandarin duck
Lanternfly
Weevil
Jewelry beetle
Tree frog
Spotted sweetlips fish
Woodboring beetle
Macaw
Betta fish
Woodboring beetle
Blue tit
Mandarin fish
Queen angelfish
Kingfisher
Boeseman's rainbowfish
Tropical fish
Butterflyfish
Sun parakeet
Hoeven's wrasse
Betta fish

Poison dart frog
Snowy owl
Monkey grasshopper
Dalmatian puppy
Comet
Stingray
Eastern baton blue butterfly
Sea slug
Egyptian green toad
Pheasar
Asian water monitor
Gecko
Coral trout
Helmeted guineafowl
Koi
Giraffe
Ladybug
Litchi bug
Gecko
Speckled kingsnake
Hyena
Cheetah
Stingray
Pygmy seahorse
Coral trout
Comet
Woodboring beetle

Spotted lady beetle
Harlequin sweetlips
Jaguar
Millennium gold discus fish
Asterope sapphira butterflies
Fire salamander
Stink bug
Butterfly
Butterfly
Longhorn beetle
Snow leopard cub
Scarab beetle
Telescope goldfish
Corn snake
Black-head snake
Leopard
Ladybug
Leopard slug
Grouper fish
Locust
Ladybug
Coral hind
Pigeon blood discus fish
Deer
Clown triggerfish
Weevil

Jumping zebra spider
Butterflyfish
Machaon caterpillar
Lemur
Emperor angelfish
Lionfish
Redknee tarantula
Emperor angelfish
Clown fish
Striped shield bug
Snail
Bongo antelope
Blue-crested lizard
Centipede
Longhorn beetle
Tiger barb
Honey bee
Zebra
Cat
Jewelry beetle
Vulturine guinea

Wasps
Woodboring beetles
Sea slug
Panther chameleon
Snout beetle
'e Bengal
'ger
Jewel scarab beetle
Checkered beetle
Striped spid
Oriental sweetlips
Woodpecker
Poison dart frog
Rosy boa
Bumblebee
Caterpillar
Sugar glider
Copperband butterflyfish
Clown surgeonfish
Zebra spider
Multibarred angelfish
iiger

Multi-colored

If you are still deciding on favorite animal color, this is the page for you. It's multi-colored mayhem!

Can you find them?

What a lot of flying colors! Can you find 3 parrots, 2 yellow butterflies, 2 blue butterflies, and 1 ladybug?

COLOR CHANGE

Chameleons can change the color of their skin! When they feel excited, the colors become brighter.

Sticker scene

Look for some multi-colored fish on your sticker sheet to add to the reef. How many can you find?

Use your stickers here!

Color me in

Color in the striped lizard.
Use as many colors as you like.

Odd one out?

One of the butterflies is slightly different.
Which one doesn't match the others?

Color Works

The three primary colors, red, yellow, and blue, can be mixed together to create all the colors of the rainbow. If you are lucky and you spot a rainbow in the sky, you will notice that the different colors blend into one another, creating a beautiful image in the sky.

In nature, animals most often match the colors around them to stay hidden, but if they were all to come out and show off, they would make a magnificent living rainbow.

The next few pages explore different animals and their amazing colors. There is an animal for every color you can imagine! And even more, there are animals of every shade of every color. How many different blues can you count? How many more can you imagine?

Let these animal rainbows inspire you to notice all the colors in the world around you.

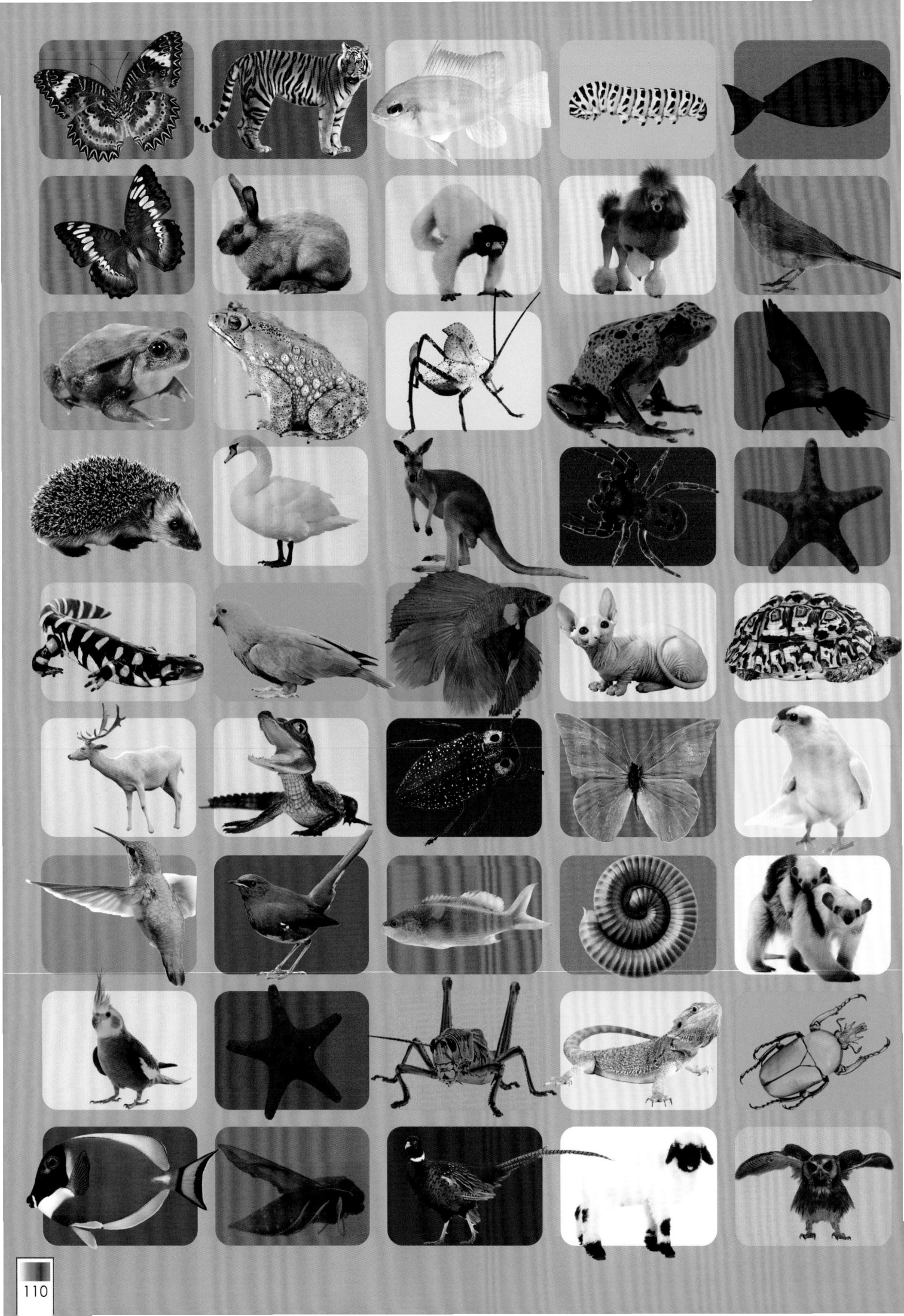